# THE WORLD'S MOST TERRIFYING PREDATORS

## PART 3

By Justin & Peter Hoke

# The World's Most Terrifying Predators Part 3

## By Justin Hoke

---

To Sam, Peter, and Joshua

---



Printed in the United States of America

First Printing, 2023

# The Black Mamba

The black mamba lives in Africa.

They eat small animals such as rodents and birds.

They are very good at using their venom to kill their prey quickly.

They can live up to 11 years.

# The Kodiak Bear

**The kodiak bear lives in Alaska.**

They eat meat, such as salmon and
other animals.

They are very strong and can run very fast.

They can live up to 25 years.

# The Golden Eagle

The golden eagle lives in North America

They eat small animals such as
rabbits and squirrels.

They are very good at flying and
swooping down to catch their prey.

They can live up to 30 years.

# The Alligator

The alligator lives in North and South America.

They eat meat, such as fish and other animals that come to drink at the river.

Alligators are very good swimmers.

They can live up to 70 years.

# The Snow Leopard

The snow leopard lives in Asia.

They eat meat, such as goats and sheep.

They are very good at climbing and can jump very far.

They can live up to 22 years.

# The Black Widow Spider

The black widow spider lives in
North America

They eat small insects and other spiders.

They are venomous and can be recognized by their black body and red hourglass shape on their abdomen.

They can live up to 3 years.

# The Komodo Dragon

The Komodo dragon lives in Indonesia.

They eat meat, such as deer and pigs.

They are the largest lizards and can run very fast.

They can live up to 30 years.

THE END